Black Hills Believables

Strange-but-true tales of the Old West

John Hafnor

Illustrated by Susan Turnbull

Library of Congress Catalog Card Number: 83-82162
ISBN 0-9648175-0-0

Manufactured in the United States of America

Published by Lone Pine Productions
Distribution and Marketing: Lone Pine Productions, 4900 Lone Pine Drive, Fort Collins, Colorado 80526, Phone (970) 223-2747

Design: Melinda MacArthur Artz

Contents

Preface

Generations of Americans have been fascinated with the story of Paha Sapa—the Black Hills of South Dakota and Wyoming. This interest has spawned a steady stream of books exploring various aspects of Black Hills history. But the little book you are about to read is different from most history books. The focus of *Black Hills Believables* is on the surprising, the nearly forgotten, the bizarre.

The collection of Believables in this book is from a promotional column appearing in the *Rapid City Journal* since December of 1979. Many of the *Journal's* readers are amateur historians, and they are some of the biggest fans of the Believables series. But these accounts are also of interest to a general readership and are written especially for the nonhistorian. Highest priority was given to presenting the stories in a colorful manner.

The subject matter is meant to be equally colorful. Where else can you unravel the mystery of Deadwood's empty graves, or read about a frontier town buried beneath a lake, or relive Babe Ruth's only Black Hills appearance? The answers are in this book.

Much of what you are about to read was uncovered here in the *Journal's* "morgue" or archive of back issues dating from our first press run on January 5, 1878. This research and the writing of each of fifty Believables in the book is by John Hafnor of the Journal. The fifty matching illustrations are by Black Hills artist Susan Turnbull.

These real-life stories remind us of what Lord Byron must have meant when he wrote, "Tis strange—but true; for truth is always strange; stranger than fiction."

James W. Swan

Publisher
The Rapid City Journal

Foreword

History should entertain. The pages of this book are meant to entertain you with accounts from the most fabled and intriguing little mountain range in America.

When regional promotors were casting about for a new name for the Black Hills ("Hills" wasn't good enough, they said, for 7,000-foot-tall mountains), Purple Mountains and Black Mountains were suggested. Magic Mountains also got a nomination. Indeed, many people consider the Black Hills to be among the most magical and mystical areas in America. This magical quality is particularly evident in the area's history, especially the period from the chaotic gold rush through the two-fisted years of early settlement.

There are many good and useful histories of the Black Hills already in print. This book is not meant to compete with the more complete volumes of Hills history. *Black Hills Believables* covers only the historical "exclamation points," with a text written in the rapid-fire style of a news flash. It is meant to be history stripped of all but the most compelling and surprising facts. Still, people unfamiliar with the region may find this outline of Black Hills events and dates to be a useful frame of reference:

10,000 B.C. to ?—Paleo-Indians inhabit at least some areas of the Hills, as surviving cliff drawings and paintings and some artifacts confirm.

1500 to 1800—Various Indian tribes inhabit the Black Hills, including Kiowa, Crow, Cheyenne and possibly Arapaho.

1743—French explorers Francois and Joseph de la Verendrye are probably the first white men to see the Black Hills.

1776—Teton Sioux begin moving into the vicinity of the Black Hills, and the Hills eventually become the center of their domain. They camp only rarely in the Hills, preferring life and hunting on the open prairie.

1800 to 1874—Occasional surveys and treks take place near the Black Hills, but mystery continues to surround what is one of the last unmapped areas in America.

1874—George Custer's thousand-man military expedition explores the interior of the Black Hills. The presence of gold is confirmed.

1874 to 1879—The gold rush years. This is the Old West's last great gold rush. Deadwood,

South Dakota, becomes the wildest and largest of the gold camps.

1886—The railroad finally arrives in Rapid City.

1890—Conflict and tragedy occur at Wounded Knee, 75 miles southeast of the Black Hills.

1890s to 1915—On the plains surrounding the Black Hills, large cattle companies utilize the open, unfenced range. This use of the country gradually yields to homesteaders and barbed wire fences.

The stories in this collection have appeared in the *Rapid City Journal* for the past three years in a column called "Black Hills Believables." Much of the inspiration for the Believables series came from observing students in Black Hills history classes at the local National College. I taught those classes, and I could not help noticing a wide-eyed enthusiasm for Hills history, especially for history stories with an unusual "twist" or a surprise ending. There seemed to be an abundance of such tales from the flamboyant Black Hills. I found more such accounts by expanding the scope of Believables to include the Badlands and other nearby points in South Dakota and Wyoming.

The Believables format does not allow for the inclusion of a great many details. That can be good or bad. It is good for people who remember high school history classes loaded with too many "boring" details. It's bad for those readers who find a Believable that fascinates them and want to know more. Those interested in greater depth have several options. Your public library may have one or more of these important books on Black Hills history: Bob Lee's *Gold-Gals-Guns-Guts*, Watson Parker's *Gold in the Black Hills*, John McClintock's *Pioneer Days in the Black Hills*, Krause and Olson's *Prelude to Glory*, or Robert Casey's *The Black Hills and Their Incredible Characters.*

Another option is to do some original research of your own. You could start with a book entitled *Dakota Visions* by David Holden. On pages 377 to 390 of this book is a long and intriguing list of points of interest. Many of the items on this list are un-researched and unexplored. There are contact people listed for each spot, people who can tell you more. It's a chance to create your own Believables!

Acknowledgments are due to many for helping with the Believables series. A partial list includes my wife, Holley; Skee and Jan Rasmussen of Belvidere, South Dakota; Cam and Doris Ferweda of Rapid City; and publisher James Swan and the rest of our staff here at the *Journal.* I should single out Sheri Fitzgerald, *Journal* librarian, who more than once tracked down information to make a Black Hills Believable believable. Artist Susan Turnbull worked especially hard at creating the historically accurate illustrations on these pages. The Rapid City Public Library has assembled an impressive collection of books on South Dakota history. It would be hard to keep coming up with Believables without that library's many shelves of Black Hills books. And I've been inspired by a woman who grew up on a badlands ranch, my mother, Marian Edwards. She taught her kids that "cowboys and Indians" were real people, with as much allure as their movie counterparts.

This collection of Believables will answer some questions, leave some questions unanswered, and hopefully create or confirm a love of history. The saga of the Black Hills is not yet finished. Neither is our combing of the past to untangle that which fascinates. There are fifty Black Hills Believables in this book, but hundreds more are hiding in libraries, attics, and the memories of Hills residents. In that you can believe.

John Hafnor

"Super Thaw" Shatters World Record

The world's greatest variance in temperature, according to the *Guiness Book of Records,* belongs to the Black Hills. It happened on a frozen Spearfish morning in 1943, with the thermometer at a bone-chilling minus four degrees. That's when the temperature shot up 49 degrees in under two minutes. So rapid was the shift in temperature that plate glass windows cracked at locations throughout town. The phenomenon was the result of a freakish chinook wind. The Indians called the wind "snow eater," but never before or since has a chinook brought such temperature contrast.

This famous chinook was unpredictable. Its winds swept over Lead, where thermometers rocketed to 52 degrees. But it missed Deadwood, less than three miles away, and that historic city still shivered in 16-below-zero weather.

The bizarre weather of January 22nd also invaded Rapid City. At mid-morning downtown Rapid City's temperature was near zero while the Canyon Lake neighborhood basked in 55 degrees. Motorists crossing from the "ice box" zone to a warmer part of town were forced to pull over—their windshields instantly obscured by a peculiar frost.

Even at the same location, the mercury would oscillate wildly. Montana-Dakota Utility's printout thermometer went from 9 degrees to 57 degrees to 10 degrees between 10:30 and 11 a.m. By noon the reading was back up to 60 degrees.

Here's part of what the *Rapid City Journal* said the next day: "The phenomenon was striking at the Alex Johnson Hotel corner at 11 a.m. On the east side of the hotel, winter was in all its glory, biting legs and faces, while around the corner on the south side, not 50 feet away, spring held sway."

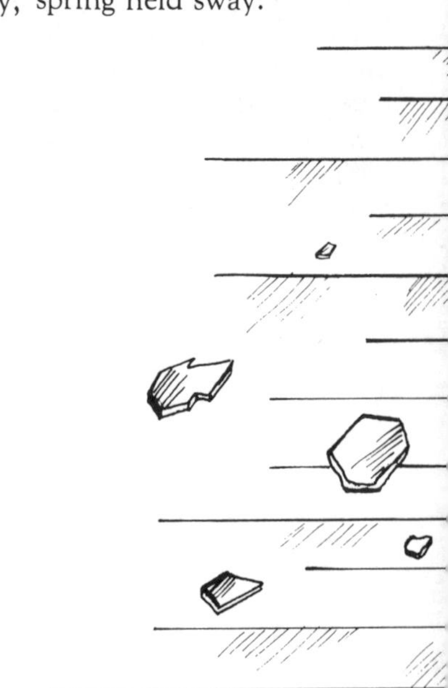

Frontier Doctor First to Climb Harney

The first white man to stand atop Harney Peak is also the first and only person ever buried up there. His name was Dr. Valentine McGillycuddy and his is the highest grave between the Rockies and the Alps!

McGillycuddy ranks as one of the Old West's forgotten heros. He arrived in the Black Hills as a combination mapmaker and surgeon with the 1875 Jenney Expedition. Just the year before, George Armstrong Custer had nearly reached the top of Harney, but could not mount the last rock rampart. McGillycuddy succeeded by felling a tall pine tree against the cliff and using it as a sort of ladder to the top.

On this same expedition McGillycuddy and two companions stumbled upon a bubbling thermal spring that spilled into a natural rock bathtub. They had unwittingly discovered the future site and namesake of the resort town of Hot Springs.

Over the years, McGillycuddy developed a special relationship with the Sioux Indians. He was one of the few white men Crazy Horse trusted. When Crazy Horse's wife became ill, the warrior sought the doctor's care at Fort Robinson, Neb. There McGillycuddy witnessed but couldn't prevent the fatal stabbing of Crazy Horse. And he was at the mystic leader's bedside throughout that long, last night.

In 1878 McGillycuddy was named chief administrator of the Pine Ridge Indian Reservation. Years later McGillycuddy moved to Rapid City, where he dabbled in banking, helped found Dakota Power Co. (now called Black Hills Power and Light), and built a home at South St. and Mt. Rushmore Road that still stands.

After the tragedy at Wounded Knee, Dr. McGillycuddy volunteered medical care for the living victims. Many were Indian women and children. He had been recalled to Pine Ridge to seek a peaceful solution to tensions arising from the Ghost Dance movement.

And McGillycuddy wasn't done showing South Dakota his breadth of talent. He would serve as president of the School of Mines, surgeon general of the territory, and as a delegate to the state's Constitutional Convention.

McGillycuddy eventually moved to California. In 1918, an influenza epidemic was sweeping America. When it reached California, the aging doctor grabbed his bag and ranged through dozens of remote communities fighting the disease. When the epidemic reached Alaska, he went there, too.

In 1939, the 90-year-old McGillycuddy died quietly. Pine Ridge's flag was lowered to half mast. The Forest Service allowed construction of a crypt in Harney's stone lookout—elevation 7,242 feet. And a pilgrimage of pioneers deposited his ashes behind a brass plaque. Thereon is listed his Indian name of Wasicu Wakan, which translates as "holy medicine man."

Cave Man has People "Petrified"

In 1892, a petrified man was discovered near the entrance to Wind Cave. Or so it was claimed. The petrified man proved to be a great hoax—probably invented by promoters of what was then a privately owned cave. Many Black Hills citizens were deceived by this stone carved fraud.

Newspapers of the day called Wind Cave's petrified man "perfect in every detail." The Hot Springs Star reported the effigy was examined by a group of physicians, who pronounced it, "...a genuine petrifaction of humanity."

The fake petrified man was put on display at the cave for a month. It was then moved to a Hot Springs sideshow tent, where for 25 cents the curious could take a peek. Then "Wind Cave Man" was exhibited throughout the country.

The "petrified man" wasn't the only publicity stunt staged at Wind Cave. In 1893, a psychic named Johnstone led a group of observers into the cave in search of a previously hidden needle. The clairvoyant found his needle alright; but must have temporarily lost his powers when he and the group became lost for two days in the cave's maze of tunnels!

The "Wind Cave Man" was certainly a deception, but a human skeleton found inside Diamond Crystal Cave was the real thing! Developers of the cave found the skeleton in 1929. They determined it to be that of a small Indian boy who fell to his death through the cave's opening 400 years ago.

The biggest of the nine Black Hills caves is Jewel Cave. It is the fourth largest cave system in the world, with 69 miles of tunnels so far discovered. Here and elsewhere cave explorers find new chambers and passages each year. These cave crawlers are the last explorers of the natural Black Hills, the last who can hope to say, "I was there first."

Some Black Hills caves may yet prove to contain over a thousand miles of passages, and if so, it may be that all the Hills' caves are connected. One theory says it might be possible to walk, or crawl, underground from Wind Cave to Deadwood. Such a journey would be made in the cool 48 degree temperature our caves maintain year around.

PETRIFIED
MAN

Report of Cross Puzzles Historians

In the heart of the Black Hills, a towering cross is said to be visible on the rock wall of a mountain. Like Colorado's more famous Mount of the Holy Cross, this Black Hills cross was first seen by frontiersmen of the last century. There are in fact two crosses, and their earliest mention is by author Edwin Curley in his pioneering *Guide to the Black Hills.* Curley wrote:

"From Custer I made the trip to the Deadwood region, passing, a few miles out, some fine mountains, which I have called Santa Cruz Peaks, because of a huge Latin cross clearly defined on a tower-like peak, and a smaller one near it. These are formed by great clefts in the rocks and seem as if chiselled out by the hand of man."

Curley penned this first-hand account in 1876, the height of the rush for Black Hills gold claims. The guide contains a miner's map listing the Santa Cruz Peaks. But the shadows and crevices forming the crosses must depend on the angle of view and time of day, as their exact location is in dispute. Take the time to scan the heights along Highway 385 on your next drive north of Custer. Perhaps you'll spot the forgotten crosses of the Santa Cruz Peaks.

Crosses based on drawings by Edwin Curley.

Living Giant was Black Hills Oldest

"The Giant is Dead," said newspaper headlines in 1972. That's when a 122-foot-tall ponderosa pine tree crashed to earth southeast of Custer. Known as the Giant of Herbert Draw, this 400-year-old tree was possibly the oldest living thing in the Black Hills. Yet it didn't die of old age.

Here was a tree that started growing in 1575, and survived the winds and fires of four centuries—a pine monarch that was already tall and healthy when the Pilgrims landed at Plymouth Rock. Yet it was laid low by a little bug, called the Mountain Pine Beetle, whose repeated infestations can kill even the biggest tree.

A forest service crew salvaged several cross-sections from the giant's trunk. One of these is on display at the Custer office of the National Forest. There you can point to the rings of the tree and see the year when Shakespeare died, or when Napoleon was born. You can see when the Hills enjoyed rainy years, or suffered through drought.

In 1981, the *Rapid City Journal's* contest to find the biggest tree in the Black Hills located other living ancients, like the Council Oak near Hermosa. Core samples from the tree, reputedly a council site for Indian tribes, indicate it may be just over 400 years old.

A most curious stand of 200-year-old trees is found near the center of the Hills. Here we find the only lodgepole pines in the region. No one is sure how they got there or why there aren't others scattered through the Hills. Some botanists call them "relic" trees—remnants of a once much larger lodgepole pine forest. Others suggest that Indians brought the lodgepole seeds here from the Bighorn Mountains. They theorize that certain tribes prized this species for the trunks which made the finest poles for a lodge or tepee.

Hikers can find the lonely lodgepole pines two miles northwest of Nahant on either side of Buskala Creek.

Rumor Triggers Stampede

If we could hear again the sounds of the 1876 gold rush, one of those sounds would be the rumble of a stampede. The biggest Black Hills stampedes were not caused by cattle or thundering buffalo, but by the prospectors themselves!

Stampedes to new diggings were fairly common in the Black Hills gold rush. Prospectors were always ready to try their luck elsewhere, and rumors of a big strike over the next hill could stampede miners in a new direction.

There were stampedes to Bear Gulch, to False Bottom Creek, and to the Bear Lodge Mountains. But strangest of all was the ill-fated Wolf Mountain Stampede.

This stampede started on the streets of Deadwood in November of 1876. Winter was coming, hay was scarce, and that meant slow times for livery stables which bought and sold horses. The one exception was Red Clark's stables, for Clark was busy buying up horses at bottom dollar.

It is now believed that Clark also arranged for an accomplice to circulate false rumors of a fabulous gold strike in the Wolf Mountains. Rumor spread like wildfire and the Wolf Mountain Stampede was on. Saddle horses were suddenly in great demand, and stable owners like Red Clark wore big smiles.

Historian Watson Parker estimates that 1,500 prospectors used countless horses in a mad dash to the Wolf Mountains. Incredible as it seems, few who joined the rush knew the exact location of the Wolf Mountains. Popular opinion held that the mountains must be in the vicinity of the distant Bighorn Range. An alleged "bald peak" was said to mark the new diggings, but neither peak nor gold was ever found.

The Wolf Mountain Stampede may have been the greatest deception in Black Hills history—perpetrated for profit on the sale of horses. In the long winter that followed, many hoaxed and haggard stampeders filtered back to Deadwood. Some returned with frozen limbs. Some never returned.

Ironic Mishap Kills Stagecoach Legend

Harvey Fellows was Deadwood's last stagecoach driver, and he set a record for longevity in the West's most glamorous job. Ironically, Fellows would safely pilot one stagecoach over 300,000 miles, only to die years later in a parade accident involving the same Concord coach.

Fellows learned the stagecoach trade at Denver in 1863. He learned to control four prancing horses on level terrain and the six horses needed for muddy or hilly conditions. Half a million miles and fifty years later, he galloped the last stagecoach over the Deadwood-Spearfish trail. That road could not be navigated by autos until 1913. Only then did the stage company switch from horses to Fords. Pioneer author John McClintock called Fellows the American recordholder for miles in a stagecoach.

In 1929 organizers of Deadwood's Day of '76 parade asked Fellows to climb aboard his old stagecoach just one more time. Feeble and nearly blind, Fellows could not drive but agreed to ride the coach. It was placed on a flatbed truck. All went well until the parade finished, and Fellows started to dismount. He had alighted from that stage a thousand times before. But this time he slipped and fell, missed the flatbed and landed hard on the ground. Harry Fellows never recovered.

Anyone who ever rode a stagecoach would smile at Hollywood's portrayal of nonstop, breakneck speed. But by yesterday's standards the stage was fast transportation, averaging a trotting pace of 6-7 mph. Fresh teams were hitched to the coach at regular intervals. We know now that stage companies saved their best team of horses for the last relay into town. And drivers were told to enter with a whoop and a holler and a galloping team!

A stagecoach was the preferred choice of transportation for those who could afford it. Even so, many passengers suffered a sort of sea-sickness as the coach rocked and rolled along.

Coaches were often official carriers of the U.S. mail, though they couldn't match the speedier pony express. One Black Hills pony express rider died in the saddle. He was Charley Nolin, ambushed by unknown gunmen at Deadman Creek.

Visits of "Sundance Kid", Twain, Ruth Nearly Forgotten

Some mighty interesting folks have passed through these Black Hills. Take Babe Ruth, for instance, who once played an exhibition baseball game here. It was 1922, and Deadwood hired Ruth to play for their team, which was hosting an all-star squad from other Hills towns. A huge crowd hung on every swing of Babe's big bat. And while the "Sultan of Swat" blasted several balls out of the park, each landed foul. Ruth did get a double and a single in three at bats, helping Deadwood to win the game.

Five years later Charles Lindbergh flew his "Spirit of St. Louis" over that same ball field. It was part of a promotion of his recent trans-Atlantic flight.

Then there was the June day in 1877 when Mark Twain dropped in to chat with fellow journalists at the "Pioneer" office in Deadwood. He was just passing through and not yet famous enough to cause much notice.

The "Sundance Kid," minus sidekick Butch Cassidy, was once in Belle Fourche just long enough to botch a holdup attempt of the Butte Co. Bank. He subsequently escaped from Deadwood's jail, hooked up with Butch Cassidy, and went on a crime spree later portrayed in a Hollywood movie.

The famed suffragist Susan B. Anthony spoke out for the female vote at Deadwood's City Hall in 1890. The speech didn't impress a young lady named Irene Cushman, who would write in her diary, "Miss Anthony is a tiresome old lady."

The first U.S. President to visit the Black Hills was William Taft in 1911. Taft was impressed with the large crowds which greeted him in Rapid City. But in truth most of the crowd was in town for another reason—to try their luck in one of the last great homestead lotteries.

Spirit of St. Louis

Landmark Earns its Eerie Name

It is said that every square yard of the Black Hills has seen a human footprint. Perhaps so...but the case could be different for the nearby Badlands. In the Badlands are flat-topped tablelands that are all but inaccessible from the surrounding land.

South of Scenic stands eerie Coffin Butte. Its crumbling 90-degree walls have been scaled only a couple of times. In 1936 a troop of Scenic Boy Scouts climbed the precipitous walls of Coffin Butte in an effort to prove or disprove an old legend. According to the old tale, 10 Indian boys ran away from the reservation. In efforts to elude a pursuing military detachment the boys supposedly formed a human bridge to the butte's summit. Soldiers surrounded the tabletop, but the boys starved rather than surrender...or so the story goes.

The Boy Scouts reached the top of Coffin Butte with the aid of telescoping ladders. There they discovered stark proof that they were not the first to scale the steep walls. They found a human skeleton. No one knows if this discovery ties in with the legend or perhaps solves one of South Dakota's "lost prospector" riddles.

The virgin grasses of most Badlands tables have waved undisturbed for centuries. Neither the buffalo nor the cow can reach these grasses. But in 1911 a severe drought caused one settler to cast a covetous eye up to the thick forage on Hay Butte. The problem was how to harvest this untapped hay crop. The answer was to pack the mower and other equipment up in pieces and then to spill the hay stacks down the side.

A similar story is told by Belvidere area rancher Skee Rasmussen, who describes how one homesteader farmed the top of a high Badlands table. This old timer planted 40 acres of corn on the butte's flat top, but to do so he had to take his tractor up there piece by piece.

Inventive ranchers could also get firewood and fence posts off the mesa tops. A long wire was stretched from the top to a post on the basin. When cut, the wood was stapled to this wire and sent scooting to the bottom. The impact of hitting the ground would knock off the staples, and the wood was ready to use!

Streets Lead to Nowhere

One hundred years ago the ground of the Black Hills cracked open and swallowed buildings...or so it seemed at Lead's Open Cut. The Open Cut is a man-made canyon hundreds of feet deep and 2,000 feet across where once stood a solid mountain. It was created when 48 million tons of rock were removed in a search for gold.

The gold ore hauled up from the Open Cut changed the map of Lead. As the gorge increased in size, Lead's business district retreated respectfully before it. North Mill Street, once the main business street, disappeared block by block as the Cut grew ever bigger. The once five-block-long street no longer exists.

Even along lower Main Street the buildings and roadway would sometimes settle a foot or more. That's because timber props that held up underground tunnels would decay in three to five years. When they gave way it was only a matter of time before big areas collapsed. In one extreme case a pair of buildings fell away into an abandoned mine cavity, leaving a pit 60 feet deep.

Shops retreated up Main Street to the present business district, where "terra firma" proved to be firmer.

The Open Cut marks the only spot where Homestake Company's famous vein of gold reached the surface. But gone are the days when Homestake could mine at or near the surface. Now deep tunnels are needed to follow the gold vein's sharp descent into the earth. North America's richest gold mine has shafts down to 8,000 feet below the Black Hills. That's 3,000 feet below either coast! And still they dig deeper.

The temperature of the rock at these depths is 134 degrees Fahrenheit. And every ton of rock yields a piece of gold only the size of a marble. Rock taken from tunnels is now replaced—a modern backfill method to prevent tunnel collapse.

Crouch Line Called Craziest Railroad

Of America's many unusual railroads perhaps none was stranger than the very short, very crooked Crouch Line in the Black Hills. This 30-mile-long railroad chugged from Rapid City to Mystic up twisting Rapid Canyon. Nearly every rail was curved to fit the canyon. A train would make the equivalent of 14 complete circles on every trip to Mystic. And people joked about the Crouch Line. They said its bends were so sharp that the brakeman on the rear car could receive a chew of tobacco from the engineer in the locomotive. They said some part of every train was always over a bridge. Indeed, there were 110 bridges on the line, or nearly four every mile.

Too many bridges—that was part of the Crouch Line's hard luck story. In 1907 a major flood demolished all but five bridges. Raging waters wrapped rails around trees and washed out most of the grade. But the plucky Crouch Line was back in service within months.

There would be other calamities in the same year. In one instance, an eastbound train plunged through a burning bridge and into the creek below. The mystery of that bridge fire was never explained. And before 1907 ended there was a thunderous collision between two engines near Big Bend.

The passing years brought more hard luck. From its birth in the early 1890s to its demise in 1947 this littlest railroad had several owners and at least 10 different names! It was variously called the Dakota & Wyoming R.R., the Dakota, Western & Missouri River R.R., the Rapid City, Black Hills & Western R.R., the Rapid Canyon Line. But Black Hills folks didn't much care for those official names. Everybody called it the "Crouch Line" for Charles D. Crouch—the man who built the railroad and who dreamed it would someday stretch to the Pacific.

Surprise Facts from the Four Faces

The Mt. Rushmore we see today is hardly the monument originally planned. Sixty years ago a sculptor was sought who could carve the Needles, not Rushmore. As planned, the Needles would become great statues of men like Fremont, or Lewis and Clark. When sculptor Gutzon Borglum arrived to view the Needles, he had a different inspiration. Borglum wanted to choose two of the granite spires and there sculpt statues of Washington and Lincoln.

Opposition sprang up to those early designs. "Man makes statues," editorialized one South Dakota newspaper, "but God made the Needles. Let them alone."

Borglum checked out other monument sites, including Harney Peak. But when he saw the "sugarloaf" dome of Mt. Rushmore, Borglum knew he'd found his mountain. The impulsive Borglum also gazed on Old Baldy, a neighboring granite summit. There, he exclaimed, was the perfect place to carve Teddy Roosevelt on horseback.

But his concentration was soon back on Rushmore. Out of its rock wall Borglum would carve great faces of Washington, Jefferson, and Lincoln. Only later did he plan the fourth face of his friend, Teddy Roosevelt.

Controversy surrounded the fourth face. Roosevelt had been dead only a few years, and some wanted more time for perspective on his presidency. In a 1969 editorial for the Los Angeles Herald-Examiner, Warren Morrell advanced an interesting theory: "It is true," wrote Morrell, "that Borglum greatly admired the Rough Rider. But look at a picture of Borglum. Put pince-nez glasses on Borglum and you have a striking resemblance to Roosevelt. So in addition to the Rough Rider, you also have Borglum up there. I don't fault him for what some might consider immodesty. I like to see Roosevelt and Borglum up there and realize I'm not seeing double."

Mt. Rushmore went through nine design changes. One example is Jefferson, originally carved on the opposite side of Washington. Faulty rock forced Borglum to literally blast the first Jefferson off the mountain, and relocate the face where we see it today.

Statehood Proposed for Black Hills

Could the Black Hills have become a separate state? One hundred and seven years ago the mineral rich Black Hills were proposed as a separate territory in a bill that reached the U.S. Senate. The movement for eventual statehood for the Black Hills was begun by unhappy miners in the gold rush days of 1876. The miners were unhappy because the capital of Dakota Territory was located at Yankton, and that remote river city proved unsympathetic to the concerns of the Hills.

The Black Hillers gained some concessions from the "Yankton Ring" by threatening to form a distinct Territory of El Dorado. The separatists later named the proposed territory Lincoln, and sent a delegate to Washington, D.C. to push their cause. Several members of Congress were interested, but a bill to create the new realm eventually failed.

When a question of admitting Dakota Territory into the Union came to the surface in 1886-89 there was again support for a separate state for the Black Hills. There was also a movement to admit the entire territory as one sprawling state. These concepts for dividing up the territory yielded to the idea of sister states called North Dakota and South Dakota. Yet it's interesting to reflect on how close we came to living in a state called Lincoln.

WELCOME
TO THE
BEAUTIFUL STATE
OF
LINCOLN

Dakota Indian Wins Olympic Gold

In 1968, Pine Ridge athlete Billy Mills captured an Olympic gold medal in the 10,000-meter run. It was the first win ever by an American in the 10,000-meter run and the first time since 1908 that an American had won any distance race in the Olympics.

Mills, an Oglala Sioux, was timed in an Olympic record 28 minutes, 24 seconds over the 6.2 mile run. He finished several paces ahead of world record-holder Ron Clarke of Australia. Mills had been considered far out of his class against one of the finest distance fields ever assembled. With a final burst of energy, he just beat Clarke and a Tunisian to the tape in what some have called the greatest upset in Olympic history. His record clocking was one minute better than his previous best time for the event.

When Mills returned from Tokyo to Pine Ridge and the Black Hills, he received a hero's welcome. The *Rapid City Journal* devoted front page coverage to his story, and carried related stories in Sports.

Mills, orphaned at an early age, became an instant symbol of Indian potential for success.

Before Mills' Olympic upset, someone had calculated his odds of winning at 1000 to 1. After the race, Olympic President Avery Brundage was moved to say, "I have been watching the Olympic Games for over 50 years and I have never seen an American athlete respond to greater pressure than Billy Mills did today in winning the 10,000 meters."

In his remaining running years, Mills would set a world record for the six mile run. But he never again approached anything like that one moment of glory in Toyko. It earned him a sort of immortality, as Pine Ridge is now known as the land of Crazy Horse, Red Cloud, and Billy Mills.

USA
722
SUSAN TURNBULL

Hills Alive with Music

The Black Hills have echoed with music since Native Americans first chanted their haunting melodies. Musical history of the Hills centers on Old Ft. Meade. It was there that "The Star Spangled Banner" received the impetus needed to later become our national anthem.

The year was 1892 and Ft. Meade Commander Caleb Carlton sought a song to be played every evening when the flag was lowered. Carlton's wife suggested "The Star Spangled Banner" and the commander agreed. From there the playing of this song became customary at every Army post each evening. Later the military anthem became the national anthem by a 1931 act of Congress. Were it not for a commander's wife at a Black Hills cavalry post, our national anthem might be "America the Beautiful" or some other tune.

At the turn of the century a bit of musical history was made at a Lead bordello called Annie's Place. The house piano player was George Norton, and he had fallen in love with Maybelle. Now history is unsure if Maybelle was a prostitute, but Norton was sure he loved her. The song which came to be known as "My Melancholy Baby" was written by Norton for Maybelle. He first scribbled it on the back of an old envelope while awaiting his love at a train depot. His lyrics were later set to music by Ernie Burnett. Norton died before "Baby" became a hit tune of World War I.

In 1874 Custer's Expedition advanced on the Black Hills bringing what must have been the first band. A mounted band was then considered essential to maintaining proper martial spirits. Custer's 16-piece band was flexible, for they could play everything from the 7th Cavalry's battle song "Gerry Owen" to a funeral dirge. They played such a dirge at services for two troopers who died in the western Black Hills.

Custer didn't bring the 7th Cavalry Band along on his next big expedition, which ended in tragedy at the Little Big Horn.

War Horses March to Pasture

The U.S. Cavalry seems to belong to the era of General Custer and Sitting Bull, yet horse-mounted cavalry troops were part of the Black Hills scene until 1942! Ft. Meade's 4th Cavalry was one of the last army units to trade its horse flesh for the vehicles of modern war. In 1939 the 4th was still an all-horse cavalry, and the fort's stables held 1,180 military mounts. Three years later only the best 480 horses remained as more and more soldiers were assigned to motorcycles and jeeps.

The war horses of Ft. Meade were unsaddled for the last time in mid-1942 as a rapidly changing U.S. Army mobilized in the Second World War. The noted F Troop was one of the last to disband. Also known as the Black Horse Troop, this group of 120 riders and black horses often performed spectacular jumping and riding drills at the Days of '76 and other rodeos.

One of military history's more celebrated horses, Comanche, was stabled at Ft. Meade. This steed was the only living survivor of Custer's Last Stand and came to the Black Hills with the famed 7th Cavalry in 1879. Comanche had been discovered two days after the battle of the Little Big Horn. The horse was riddled with bullet wounds, but a decision was made to nurse him back to health. The 7th Cavalry thereafter reserved for Comanche a strictly ceremonial and parade existence. By special order this horse was never again ridden or worked. Today an important street at Ft. Meade is named for Comanche.

Nation's "Bull's Eye" Near Black Hills

For generations the accepted center of the United States was a monument in north-central Kansas. The addition of Alaska, by mathematical wizardry, shifted the nation's center to Butte County, South Dakota. With the addition of Hawaii, it was again relocated a few miles to the southwest at a point 21 miles north of Belle Fourche. A plaque on Highway 85 proclaims that spot the "Center of the United States."

South Dakota has also claimed to be the center of the North American continent. A monument on Snake Butte, just north of Pierre, is said to be the center of South Dakota, as well as the approximate center of North America. The plaque specifically says "approximate center," and admits that a National Geographic study gives the center of the continent to Rugby, North Dakota. The engraving ends by saying that the location of the geographical center is open to debate, depending on which of several methods are used in figuring it. The National Geographic's method didn't account for bodies of water, like Hudson Bay.

We do know that South Dakota is as far away from a salt water sea as one can get on this continent. That fact was used to name a valley near Custer as America Center, for the center of North America. The Black Hills country is the continental "heartland," and that is one reason why it remained one of the last unexplored, unmapped areas in the 48 United States. The interior of the Black Hills was largely unmapped until the middle 1870s—a time when most of the rest of our nation was crisscrossed with roads and ribbons of rail.

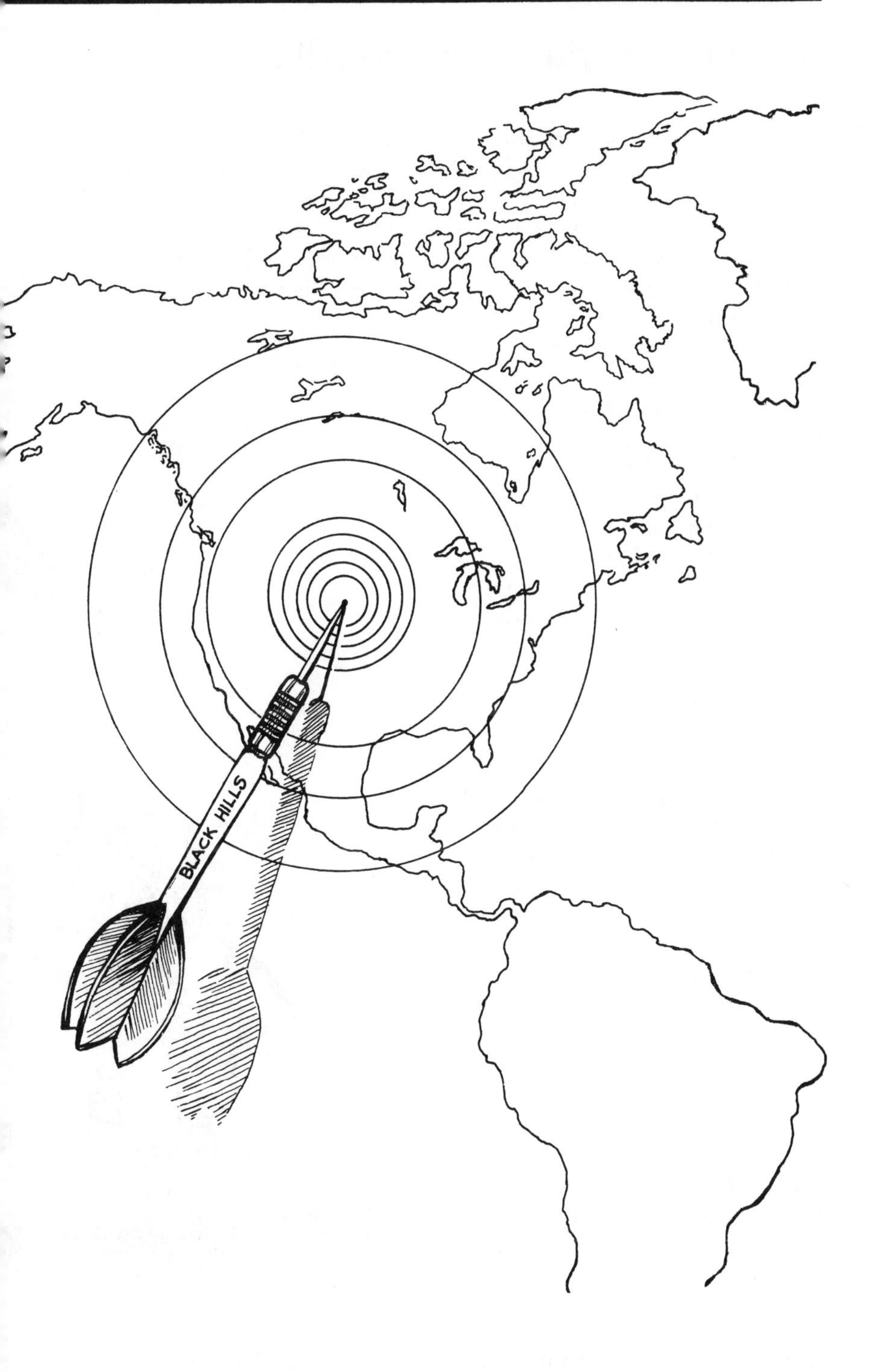
BLACK HILLS

Settler's Dispute was Needless

One of the strangest county seat wars was waged in the Black Hills. Like frontier towns everywhere, both Custer City and Hayward wanted the county seat. Years later surveyors discovered that the two were actually located in different counties!

In 1877 a newly appointed board of commissioners met in Custer City and organized Custer County. The county capital was soon moved from Custer City to Hayward, however, because it was bigger. Hayward's population, mostly miners, was about 300.

Hayward remained the temporary county seat until an election was held to permanently locate the capital. Custer claimed the election. Hayward refused to concede, saying many fraudulent votes were cast. For two years feelings ran high and things occasionally got rough. Contact between the two towns often resulted in fisticuffs or worse.

In 1879 Custer finally won out over the loud protestations of a dwindling Hayward. In 1881 surveyors definitely fixed the boundary between Custer and Pennington counties. They discovered the towns weren't even in the same county. While Custer City was smack in the middle of Custer County, Hayward was two miles inside the Pennington County line! Today Custer is a prosperous community of 2,000 while Hayward is a near ghost town.

Sister States Battle for Sitting Bull's Grave

The proposed dimensions of the Crazy Horse memorial are staggering. At 563 feet high it will be taller than the Washington Monument. The length will be 641 feet, and that's longer than two football fields. Crazy Horse's head will be 87½ feet tall, which is equivalent to Rushmore's Washington head, plus Miss Liberty's head, plus an additional 10½ feet.

Sculptor Korczak Ziolkowski didn't always deal in such heroic proportions. One of his smaller works is a bust that marks Sitting Bull's grave near Mobridge. Below are some curious historical facts concerning this grave.

Sitting Bull was born and died on South Dakota soil, but he was initially buried across the North Dakota border at Fort Yates. For many years Sitting Bull's remains lay forgotten in the North Dakota graveyard. In 1953 a group of historically motivated individuals, led by Clarence Grey Eagle, sought to have the great Sioux leader's remains brought back to South Dakota.

Sitting Bull's surviving relatives agreed with the plan. But negotiations with the governors of North and South Dakota and other prominent officials repeatedly broke down. Both states wanted Sitting Bull's grave!

On April 8, 1953, Grey Eagle and friends could wait no longer. In a dramatic midnight raid on the North Dakota graveyard, involving several vehicles, a backhoe and an airplane, Sitting Bull's bones were secretly dug up.

The remains were soon back in South Dakota. To assure that North Dakotans wouldn't steal the bones back, they were encased in a concrete block weighing 20 tons. The bizarre story received national and international coverage. South Dakota's Governor Anderson said he approved of the return of the bones, but frowned on the method used. North Dakotans called it grave robbery.

Roosevelt said, "Bully for Bullock!"

They were big men, and they named mountains for each other. Teddy Roosevelt and Deadwood's first sheriff, Seth Bullock, were a couple of bigger-than-life individuals who first met on the plains of Dakota in 1884. They were fast friends until both died within a few months of each other in 1919.

President Roosevelt cemented his friendship with Bullock by seeing to it that Scruton Peak, south of Pactola, was renamed "Seth Bullock Peak." The fire lookout on top of this 6,000-foot peak can be seen from parts of Rapid City on a clear day.

When Teddy Roosevelt died Seth Bullock led a frenzied drive to erect a tower monument for him on Sheep Mountain. That peak is about four miles north of Deadwood, and was soon named Mount Roosevelt. The monument was the first in the United States dedicated to Roosevelt.

Teddy thought so much of Seth Bullock that he sent his sons to the Bullock Ranch to change them from "tenderfeet" into "cowboys." Roosevelt often boasted of Seth as being "my typical ideal American."

The record shows that Bullock cleaned up Deadwood in the 1870s without ever gunning down a single offender. Instead he relied on his wits and extremely strong personality.

Some of Bullock's other accomplishments—he is credited with introducing and promoting the crop of alfalfa in South Dakota. As a member of the Montana Territorial Senate he wrote the resolution that eventually resulted in Congress establishing Yellowstone National Park. Seth was commissioned captain of the Spanish-American War era unit known as Grigsby's Cowboys or the Black Hills Rough Riders. He was appointed first supervisor of the Black Hills National Forest by Roosevelt. He was also a successful merchant, lecturer and statesman.

Bullock had two final requests. One was that he be buried so high up on Deadwood's "Boot Hill" that one could gaze north and see the tower monument on Mount Roosevelt. His other request was that instead of an epitaph his tombstone carry only the single word, "Pioneer."

SHERIFF
SUSAN TURNBULL

War Declared at Gas Stations

In the summer of 1923 gas topped 29 cents a gallon in Rapid City. That price seems like a bargain now, but by the standards of the day anything over 20 cents a gallon was considered exorbitant.

South Dakota's governor was then Bill McMaster. He responded to the high gas prices by ordering the state highway department to begin selling gas at all its district offices for 16 cents a gallon. McMaster directed state officials to buy gasoline in Chicago and ship it by tank car to Rapid City and Deadwood in addition to seven East River cities.

The oil companies were outraged, and cries of "socialism" were heard. But the "Governor's Gas War" was successful in forcing prices down at commercial pumps. Thereafter every time the gas stations tried to raise their prices the Republican McMaster responded with another state sale.

South Dakota's war on high gas prices received nation-wide attention and triggered price reductions throughout the Midwest and eventully from coast to coast. An Associated Press story of 1923, dateline Chicago, said, "The whole gasoline price evolves about the South Dakota situation, as it did when the original reduction made Monday was followed by price cuts in all parts of the country."

Motorists were delighted with the low prices. South Dakota's politicians involved the state in several other projects normally reserved for the private sector. They initiated state ownership of a cement plant, a coal mine, and several grain elevators.

The U.S. Supreme Court finally stepped in and ruled that selling gas was not a proper function of state government.

GAS
GAS
.29
.16¢
SUSAN TURNBULL

Ancient Black Hills are Mountains in Decline

There are no mountains on the North American continent older than our Black Hills range. The ancient origin of the Hills was documented by analysis of a granite outcropping found north of Nemo. Test results revealed the Black Hills to be 2.5 billion years old! Through the eons these primordial Hills were worn down to a nearly level surface. Then new uplifts, beginning 600 million years ago, created the present-day peaks.

These Black Hills were called Paha Sapa by the Sioux Indians. They might be known today as the Black Mountains but for a curious feature of the Sioux language. The Hills were sighted by the westward-moving Oglala Sioux around the year 1776. It was then that the slopes were named for their dark appearance when viewed from afar. Sapa is the Lakota word for "Black." But that language then used the single word Paha for any height, be it mountain or hill.

In the early 1800s Paha Sapa was translated as "Black Mountains." But by the time of the gold rush this area was most frequently called the Black Hills. A popular ballad of that period ends as follows:

On their backs are no clothes,
in their pockets no bills,
Each day they keep starting
for the dreary Black Hills.

Mt. Rushmore Story is Unfinished

Mt. Rushmore has four familiar faces, but could there have been five? Sculptor Gutzon Borglum was happy with his carving of four presidents. Others, however, clamored for a fifth great face.

In 1937 a bill was introduced to Congress attempting to add Susan B. Anthony to Mt. Rushmore. Borglum was repeatedly asked why this women's rights crusader could not be among the faces on Rushmore. His response to this and all other calls for a fifth face was always the same: There was simply not enough good, unfaulted granite remaining.

This didn't stop others, including a young senator named Hubert Humphrey. In 1949 Humphrey's resolution to Congress asked for the addition of Franklin Roosevelt to Rushmore. Years earlier Roosevelt had hosted a White House luncheon for sculptor Borglum. During the meal Borglum casually sketched his Mt. Rushmore as the President watched. Jokingly or not, Borglum penciled in a fifth face among his famous four—Franklin Roosevelt's. Borglum made no promises and Roosevelt did not comment on the sketch. But some claimed that Borglum later found federal funds easier to obtain.

In 1963 private individuals suggested that slain President John Kennedy become the fifth stone face. Similar rumblings were heard when Eisenhower died in 1969.

More recently an Italian camera crew claimed to see a fifth face in their exposed film. It looked like the profile of an Indian male. With a strong imagination and proper lighting you too may see this unintended fifth face below Washington.

The four faces of Rushmore are not finished. Some detail work remains on Roosevelt's face. Borglum once said, "The head of Washington will be continued on down to the knees...." Then there is Lincoln's hand, just below his chin. Most find that unfinished hand unrecognizable. Borglum had also planned a "Grand Stairway" up the mountain, one that would rival the steps of the Acropolis. This mighty stairway would have taken visitors up very near Lincoln's head and hand. The

National Park Service felt the stairs were both too risky for visitors and too expensive for government. All climbing is currently prohibited at Rushmore though in the 1930s tour guides regularly led visitors to the top.

Miller's Peak Shares Secrets

There's a little peak in the Black Hills that contains some mighty big history. It is sometimes called Piedmont Butte (so says the U.S. Geological Survey) and sometimes Miller's Peak (so named by old-timers after a nearby homestead).

On the butte's slopes scientists uncovered the fossilized bones of a new species of dinosaur. John Honerkamp's book *At the Foot of the Mountain* details the discovery of the 50-ton prehistoric lizard. Excavation was performed by Professor O.C. Marsh, a man associated with both Yale University and the Smithsonian Institution. Marsh named his Piedmont beast the "Barosaurus."

Several historic expeditions have passed within the shadow of Piedmont Butte. In 1857 Lt. Warren and party passed close to the butte while mapping the perimeter of the Black Hills. The 1,000-man Custer Expedition of 1874 exited the Hills where Elk Creek runs beside Piedmont Butte. A few months later the gold-seeking Gordon Party sneaked into the Hills past Piedmont Butte. They then camped a mile or so south of the peak.

In the early 1900s, Fort Meade's mounted troopers occasionally used the slopes on and around Piedmont Butte to practice maneuvers and mock cavalry charges. Early settlers found a fine petrified forest on the eastern slope, an attraction we now call the Black Hills Petrified Forest.

It's easy to see Piedmont Butte—look for the solitary peak that sits less than one mile east of 1-90 at Piedmont. You'll be viewing a little mountain with a history to compare with Harney and other lofty peaks.

Ghost Towns Seem to Vanish

Towns can't just disappear...or can they? Old maps of the Black Hills are speckled with boom towns and mining camps that flourished—then faded. Historians aren't even sure where some sizable communities were located.

Take the case of American City. This town reportedly was located somewhere in or near Spearfish Canyon. Time and flood waters have removed all traces of the town, and nothing else is known about its location.

Early newspaper accounts tell us there were three adjoining villages known as Beaver City, Quartz City and New Berlin. These hamlets were home to 150 miners. The best guess is that the remains of these ghost towns are somewhere between Nemo and Roubaix Lake.

These and over 500 other ghost towns are listed in the interesting book *Black Hills Ghost Towns*, by Watson Parker and Hugh Lambert. More than a dozen of the towns have no known location.

Canyon Springs was a stagecoach relay station somewhere east of Four Corners, Wyoming. It was at Canyon Springs in 1878 that outlaws ambushed a stage and its cargo of $100,000 in Homestake gold. Three of the robbers died in a hail of gunfire from Homestake guards. But at least two of the bandits escaped with the loot, though in their hasty retreat they dropped one of the gold bars. Another of the gold bars eventually turned up in Iowa. The rest was never found. The location of that gold, and of Canyon Springs, has been a topic of debate every since.

Another puzzler is the wild railhead town named Whoop-up, which seems to have been located near Newcastle. We know only that Whoop-up lasted just one year. Then it was moved lock, stock and barrel to nearby Tubb Town.

Postage records show that Centennial City's post office served 52 people. But where was Centennial City? The whereabouts of Saratoga is also in question. A very inaccurate map from 1883 shows Saratoga southwest of Sturgis, roughly where Boulder Park is today.

These and other examples prove that Black Hills history is a fascinating and yet unfinished mosaic.

CANYON SPRINGS
1 MILE

Boom Towns Quickly Go "Bust"

The Black Hills gold rush was the last great gold rush in the continental United States. Its colorful nature often makes us forget the silver "boom," and the tin "boom," and others that followed. These boom and bust cycles, and fluctuating prices for minerals, combined to create many Black Hills ghost towns.

Besides gold, silver and tin, here are the mined minerals that had promoters calling our Black Hills the "richest hundred miles square on earth!"—copper, mica, coal, tungsten, lead, graphite, gypsum, feldspar, Fuller's earth and jamesonite. There was even some time spent prospecting for diamonds, though to no avail.

History records some spectacular population shifts in the Black Hills mining camps. Custer experienced an almost overnight depopulation when richer placers were found to the north. The same thing happened to Hill City. Some accounts claim that both Custer and Hill City went from populations in the thousands to a mere handful who remained to guard property.

Then there was the case of Crook City. You can reach what is left of this one-time city of 2,000-3,000 people by going about a mile south of Whitewood. In 1876 Crook City was growing by leaps and bounds. One reporter noted that, of 250 buildings in town, at least half were saloons. But there was also a school, a church and other civic buildings. Curiously, the Crook City Tribune came out with a first issue on June 10, 1876, but was never published again.

Crook City collapsed almost as fast as it grew. When bypassed by the Fremont, Elkhorn and Missouri Valley Railroad, the folks of Crook City started leaving. They took their possessions and even some buildings with them. By the early 1880s most of Crook City was empty enough to be homesteaded by a pair of individuals. In 1900 the census showed just 27 souls in once mighty Crook City.

Pioneer Preacher Faithful to the End

In 1876 Deadwood was as loud and lawless as any mining camp in the American West. But amidst the gunfire and dust and profanity stood "Preacher" Smith, a symbol of more peaceful times to come. Reverend Henry Smith was a Methodist minister who held his first Deadwood services at the corner of Main and Gold streets on Sunday, July 9, 1876. Most of his preaching was in the open-air.

Those who were there said it was not uncommon to see Preacher Smith holding the attention of one end of the crowd while at the other end a gambler or salesman shouted at the same motley throng. Smith also preached in a sawdust-floored log house in Custer City and in other Hills camps. He supported himself with part-time jobs.

The real life legend of Preacher Smith ended on August 20, 1876, when he attempted to walk from Deadwood to Crook City to hold services. As always, he had answered those concerned for his personal safety by saying the Bible would be his protection. Smith had proceeded only a few miles from Deadwood when he was shot by an unknown assassin. He was buried up on Deadwood's "Boot Hill" cemetery, but a monument stands along Highway 14-85 at the point where the 49-year-old religious man died.

SALOON
SUPPLIES

Lions and Bears—Fact or Fancy?

The roarings of bears and mountain lions have echoed through the Black Hills for centuries. Some claim these mighty predators still roam the Hills.

In 1874 George Custer shot a grizzly bear near his Army camp 10 miles north of present day Deerfield. Later he immodestly wrote to his wife about the accomplishment, saying, "I have reached the hunter's highest round of fame."

There were many other written and photographic records attesting to the former existence of Black Hills bears and cougars. Most people now agree that both species are extinct in the Black Hills. But in the last decade there have been some intriguing eye witness reports of bears and cougars.

A few years ago Dr. Sven Froiland authored *Natural History of the Black Hills,* in which he lists both black bears and cougars in the "extremely rare" category.

Over the years an occasional cougar or bear has escaped from local zoos or tourist attractions. For Ted Schenck, wildlife specialist with the Game, Fish and Parks Department, these fugitives merely muddle the issue. He is convinced that we have a small and native reproducing population of Hills cougars but doubts the claims for Black Hills bears.

Bear Country, U.S.A. owner "Doc" Casey agrees that wild bears in the Hills are, "a possibility but not a probability." Nonetheless, Casey tells some stories that are hard to explain. In one incident, in 1973, a man living on Iron Mountain Road phoned Casey to complain about what he said was a bear tipping over the garbage cans. Casey listened to the man's detailed description of the animal, then dispatched an employee to count his Bear Country inmates. The bear census showed that none of Casey's animals were missing. So what was the big animal on Iron Mountain Road?

Sliced Bacon

Mystical Mountain is Loaded with Legend

Many of the world's religions carry the story of a great flood. In the Bible it was Noah and his ark who came to rest on Mt. Ararat. For the religious Mandan Indians the only man saved from a similar global flood brought his great canoe to rest on top of Bear Butte in the Black Hills.

Other tribes have contributed to Bear Butte's status as a religious shrine. For the Cheyenne Indians the butte is a kind of American Mecca, and annual pilgrimages are still made to the mountain. Over the centuries Bear Butte has served as a watchtower and as a landmark. Its vegetation was several times set on fire, either to serve as a beacon or to dislodge enemies.

In 1857, Bear Butte was the site of the largest known gathering of Sioux Indians. This Great Council established the policy of holding the Black Hills against white encroachment.

The most peculiar aspect of the butte is the stones found in the forks of its trees. These stones were placed there by Indians as a form of worship or good luck, or possibly as a system of communication. Frontier author Pete Rosen wrote about the ingrown stones in 1883 and estimated that they had been placed there 40 years prior. By hiking to Bear Butte's summit, one can still see the unusual stones in the trees.

For the white man Bear Butte was a junction for three historic trails, and two-thirds of the miners swarming to the Hills passed by the butte.

For a time the city of Sturgis conducted caravans of tourists to the summit astride sturdy little burros. Geologists tell us that Bear Butte was formed by volcanic pressures but that eruptions similar to those on Mt. Saint Helens are not possible.

"Holy Terror" and Other Names are Funny, Fitting

What's in a name? In the Black Hills, curious and interesting stories lurk behind many names. Take the case of Nemo. This village was named by a superstitious prospector who thought it was a good omen when a lump of quartz rolled down the hill in front of him. To keep from changing his luck, the miner spelled "omen" backwards when naming his townsite.

False Bottom Creek got its name in the summer of 1876. Before then it was just another nameless creek north of Central City. This creek had been thoroughly prospected down to bedrock, but little gold was found. Then a rumor sprang up that the bedrock under the creek was only a "false bottom." Riches were said to await those who dug still deeper. Miners stampeded back to the creek. But still no gold was found in what has since been called False Bottom Creek.

The Homestake Mine was named by miners who only hoped they had staked out a claim big enough to pay their way back home. Perhaps they even dreamed of a stake that would buy a new home. But their Homestake turned out to be so much more—the Western Hemisphere's biggest gold mine.

The town of Buffalo Gap is named for a nearby gap in the Hills. Through this canyon great herds of buffalo migrated from the plains into the grasslands of today's Wind Cave and Custer parks. Evidence of this "buffalo highway" is still visible.

The Holy Terror Mine of Keystone was discovered in 1894. The owner, a man with a sense of humor, always said he named the mine after his wife.

Finally, there is Hisega, a community established in 1908. It is a name dreamed up by six young girls who picnicked at the site. Their names were Helen, Ida, Sadie, Ethel, Grace and Ada. The initials of those names spell HISEGA.

HELEN
IDA
SADIE
ETHEL
GRACE
ADA

Modern Lakes Submerge Frontier Towns

The gold rush towns of Sheridan and Pactola were born in 1875. Today both lie buried in watery graves—at the bottom of lakes that bear their names.

None of the Black Hills' lakes existed when the gold rush of 1876 occurred. All are man-made, from spacious Angostura to pint-sized Sylvan Lake. At Pactola and Sheridan lakes the '76ers would be mighty surprised to learn that their towns are now visited only by scuba divers!

Rapid City scuba divers Andy Hofmann, Ray Lucan and Mike Hall have all brought back reports from the bottom of Pactola Lake. They can tell you about following the submerged road down from the north boat landing. They know the road leads towards old Pactola...past an underwater bridge...and among tree trunks that haven't yet toppled. They can show other divers an old stone powder house and swim in and out of its doors and windows.

At depths over 100 feet divers approach the remains of Pactola—mostly just foundations and faintly visible streets. Silt is covering up everything, including a big rock on which names were lovingly carved many years ago. Pactola took its name from the mythical Pactolus, a river with sands of gold. But for a time, it was called "O" Valley, after the beautifully round basin in which it is located. That setting made Pactola the perfect spot for a dam and reservoir.

Sheridan, like Pactola, was a boom town. At one time it was the temporary Pennington County seat, home of the U.S. Land Office, and site of the Black Hills Circuit Court.

When the gold dwindled, so did both Sheridan and Pactola. A dam was completed at Sheridan in the 1940s. Planners named the new reservoir "Lake of the Pines," but folks preferred to call it Sheridan Lake. A decade later the 220-foot-tall Pectola Dam was completed. Most buildings were moved to higher ground.

Pactola and Sheridan aren't the only Black Hills lakes to flood historical sites. The waters of Deerfield Lake cover an important campsite of George Custer's 1874 expedition to the Black Hills.

POWDER

Great Flood Left Question Marks

There is a legend of a Black Hills flood so terrible that it would dwarf even the great floods of 1883, 1907, and 1972. Called the B.C. (Before Custer) flood, it occurred before the arrival of General Custer and white settlement. Just when this flood happened no one can be sure. But evidence of the great deluge can still be seen at Boulder Canyon near Sturgis and Little Elk Canyon by Piedmont. Scattered east of these canyons are huge car-sized rocks, thought to have been carried out of the canyons by a flood of terrifying power. Some of the great stones were pushed half a mile or more.

Frank Thomson wrote of the B.C. flood in his little book *Last Buffalo of the Black Hills.* Thomson's theory was that a great flood exterminated buffalo from the central Black Hills. His guess was that the flood happened in 1852, and for him it explained why early settlers found buffalo skulls in the Hills, but no living buffalo.

Thomson's study was long on speculation and short on historical evidence. But there are other accounts suggesting a catastrophic flood. The Sioux Indian Chris Colome related a story told to him by relatives. "During the early 1850s," said Colome, "there came a mighty winter such as no Indian had ever seen before. Snow piled up to 30 feet deep." A record snowfall like that could have caused flooding, especially if quickly thawed by warm rains. And deeply drifted snow might explain why pioneers saw stumps of trees cut off nine feet above the ground, or why an elk skull was once discovered 25 feet high in the forks of a pine.

Amidst the lack of hard evidence, this much we know: Deep in the Black Hills past was a great flood witnessed by few and recorded by none.

Wanted: House Cats for Cat Houses!

Before railroads, all freight was hauled to the frontier Black Hills in wagons pulled by long rows of oxen or mules. The most famous wagon of freight came loaded with crate after crate of house cats!

It seems that Deadwood in 1876 had no cats. This feline shortage was especially noticed by the dance hall girls and "fallen women" who sought cats as both pets and mouse catchers. Mule skinner Phatty Thompson's idea was to fill the void with a wagon load of cats from Cheyenne. And Thompson, a big coarse man with a soft heart, proved he could be a shrewd businessman.

Once in Cheyenne Phatty told the young boys of town that he would pay 25 cents for each cat they could catch and bring to him. It wasn't long before Thompson's wagon was full of noisy alley cats. On the long trip to Deadwood there was a single mishap—the wagon overturned while crossing Spring Creek near Hill City. Most of the cats escaped.

With the help of some nearby prospectors Thompson coaxed all but one of his living cargo back into their crates. It took about 12 days of travel for a freight wagon to travel from Cheyenne to the Hills.

Once on the streets of Deadwood Thompson had no trouble finding buyers. He sold the cats by the pound. Accounts say the fattest cats brought as much as $20-$30, and Thompson pocketed nearly a thousand dollars.

Some have suggested that the name "cat house" for a house of prostitution may have arisen from this incident. Eric Partridge's *Dictionary of Slang* suggests otherwise. Whatever the case, the true story of the cat cargo proves again how much people love their pets.

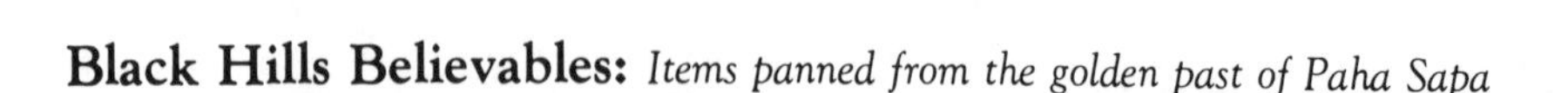

Wild Bill was Master of Deadwood Gunmen

In 1876 Deadwood earned its reputation as a "wide open" town. Many came who had no intention of toiling in the gold fields. For America's gamblers, gunmen and con artists, the word was "Deadwood."

Ironically history tells us little of the lives of pick and shovel miners, but much of the exploits of the Wild Bill Hickoks and the Calamity Janes. We know of visits to the Black Hills by many other Western figures, including Wyatt Earp, Bat Masterson, Buffalo Bill, Sam Bass and the Sundance Kid.

Our conception of these notables is a strange mixture of fact and myth. Take the case of Wild Bill Hickok. His fame can be traced to a highly exaggerated Harper's Monthly article printed in the late 1860s. He was known then, less glamorously, as Duck Bill Hickok.

In the book *Gold in the Black Hills*, historian Watson Parker writes of Hickok as "...a gambler, part-time gunman, and full-time liar who worked in all three professions."

Hickok's place in history was guaranteed by the dramatics of his assassination. It's said the "Prince of Pistoleers" never sat with his back to the door, but he was doing just that while playing cards on August 2, 1876. This allowed the vagrant Jack McCall to approach the 39-year-old Wild Bill unseen and shoot him in the head at point-blank range.

McCall then tried to shoot the other players but his gun misfired. Hickok was killed almost instantly, but tradition tells us he had both guns out and cocked before slumping over the table. Before him lay the cards which are to this day famous as the "deadman's hand"...black aces and eights, and the Jack of Diamonds.

McCall was tried and acquitted in Deadwood by a people's court. He would later hang from the gallows in Yankton for the same offense.

Mountain Men Kindled Hills Legends

The real-life story of Jedediah Strong Smith began in 1823 when his party of explorers and trappers made the first recorded passage over the Black Hills. It was Jed Smith's earliest far-western expedition, and started at Fort Kiowa near present-day Chamberlain. Having but few horses, the mountaineers were forced to walk up the White River to that opening in the Hills called Buffalo Gap. They entered into what one member described as "...a pleasant undulating pine region, cool and refreshing, so different from the hot dusty plains we have been so long passing over." Hot, indeed. Between the White River and the Hills, one dehydrated trapper was intentionally but temporarily buried up to his neck in moist soil, thus giving others time to search for water.

The explorers pushed westward and may have crossed what is now Wind Cave National Park. Somewhere along the trail Jed Smith was attacked by a grizzly bear and his scalp was half torn off. Companions did a very rough job of sewing the scalp back in place. Thereafter Smith wore his hair long to conceal frightful scars.

One of the traditional tall tales of the mountain men, that of a standing petrified forest, originated with this expedition. This wild tale inspired Edgar Allen Poe to write of a "petrified forest near the head waters of the Cheyenne River which has its source in the Black Hills." An overly enthusiastic edition of the *St. Louis Press* said the forest's branches held small petrified birds!

Jedediah Smith went on to fame as the West's most intrepid mountain man, but he never forgot his struggles in Paha Sapa.

Hard Riding Scout had Romantic Heart

Captain Jack Crawford was a rough-hewn explorer of the Black Hills, a soldier of fortune, and a sidekick of Buffalo Bill Cody and Wild Bill Hickok. He also wrote beautiful poetry.

Captain Jack gained fame as the "Poet Scout," but he never planned it that way. Until the Civil War, Crawford was illiterate. Battle wounds put him in a Union hospital and while there a nurse taught him to read and write.

In 1875 Captain Jack came to the Black Hills as a reporter for the *New York Herald* and may have been the region's first newspaper correspondent. He reached the Hills on a horse loaned to him by Joseph Gossage of Sidney, Nebraska. Gossage later founded the *Rapid City Journal.*

Captain Jack was chief of scouts under General Crook during the Battle of the Little Big Horn. It's said that Jack was riding to Custer's headquarters with dispatches when the 7th Cavalry was wiped out. Later the "Poet Scout" toured with Buffalo Bill's Wild West Show. Through it all he kept composing poems and plays.

After an absence of several years, Captain Jack made his last visit to Rapid City in 1893. He liked the town, and dedicated a poem to his "Foot Hills Queen." Captain Jack was dismayed at how fast things were changing, and ended the poem with this warning:

Remember Rome was not erected in a day
You may be Rapid, yet I thought it strange
That some were roaring for a rabid change
Sustain the good old name while time shall last
Be Rapid always—
but be not too fast.

Indian Mystery is Modern Puzzle

The first mountain men and explorers to visit the Black Hills reported hearing strange and unexplainable booming sounds. The mystery of these underground rumblings remains to this day. Nearly every explorer to visit the Hills prior to 1833 makes reference to the strange roar, a sound which was often compared to the discharge of cannons. There is general agreement that these noises, often heard on cloudless days, did not refer to thunder.

These early boomings and reverberations endowed the Black Hills with an aura of intrigue and mystery for Indians and white men alike. Lewis and Clark never reached the Black Hills country, but learned of this area from the fur trapper Jean Valle. Referring to these heights as the Black Mountains, Valle said, "...a great noise is heard frequently from these mountains."

A possible explanation for the phenomenon was advanced by Hyman Palais in 1941. In the *Black Hills Engineer* Palais wrote "These strange rumblings have been attributed to the escape of hydrogen from subterranean beds of burning coal. No visitors to the regions where these noises had been heard fail to mention the curious phenomenon. After the year 1833 the rumblings evidently ceased, for explorers no longer mention hearing them." Yet there has never been a documented and satisfactory explanation. The Black Hills mystery of the great noise remains for us to ponder.

SUSAN
TURNBULL

The White Cavalry—America's Snow Fighters

In 1941 Black Hills residents could witness a curious mixture of skis, horses, machine guns, snow shoes and soldiers. It all added up to the only cavalry snow troop in America, and was an experimental unit of Ft. Meade's 4th Cavalry. In sub-zero temperatures the horsemen resurrected and improved the winter fighting lessons learned by both Indians and cavalrymen in the 1800s.

From a winter bivouack near Hanna in the Northern Hills, white-uniformed troopers conducted maneuvers on horseback. Once dismounted they proceeded over the snow on skis or snow shoes. Reports from the time said troopers always advanced in a staggered line to better blend in with the snow.

By 1941 the days of the classic cavalry charge were long gone. But the Army still felt horses had some value in modern warfare. The horse was used as a sort of "all terrain vehicle" and as a mount for scouting units.

The snow troops of the Black Hills combined traditional horse power with the mechanized variety. Huge semi-trailers were used for transportation behind the lines. Each truck carried eight cavalrymen and eight horses. The troopers were spending more time with scout cars and motorcycles and less time with horses.

As might be expected the vehicles experienced normal "slipping and sliding" problems on the snowy meadows. These problems were reported in a March 4, 1941, article in the *Rapid City Journal.* The final line of that article reflected this lingering bias for the horse—"But after all it is the man on horse who excels under all conditions of terrain and weather."

Nations Pondered Black Hills Offer

Just after World War II the United Nations was looking for a permanent headquarters. The site chosen was to become a sort of "world's capital city." The Black Hills area was seriously considered. South Dakota's Governor Sharp joined the governors of Wyoming and Nebraska in formally inviting the United Nations to locate in the Black Hills. Senators and congressmen pushed the plan, as did a local committee headed by Rapid City dynamo Paul Bellamy.

Press releases from around the world mentioned the Black Hills alongside candidate cities like Geneva, Brussels and Philadelphia, where an editorial in the Inquirer said, "The Black Hills must be recognized as real competition."

When Paul Bellamy flew to London to represent the Hills before a site selection committee, Time magazine said, "The star performer was Paul Bellamy, a bull-necked businessman who represents no city, but the bleak Black Hills of South Dakota where men are men and steaks are three inches thick."

The bid to establish the United Nations in the Black Hills was more than just a publicity stunt. Promoters were well armed with arguments. They said the Black Hills offered an opportunity to build a U.N. Peace Capital from scratch—and where no large city would absorb the capital's identity. Maps were issued showing the Black Hills as the most equally convenient location by air to all nations. Governor Sharp even offered to declare a 10-mile square "District of the World" where the state would yield sovereignty.

Bellamy wanted to see the name Black Hills changed to Black Mountains. He didn't feel "hills" properly described the grandeur of the area. In London Bellamy had a hard time convincing some of the delegates that the Hills "...were not just little piles of black dirt."

Greece became the first nation to endorse the Black Hills site, but none others followed. New York City easily won the vote as the new home of the U.N.

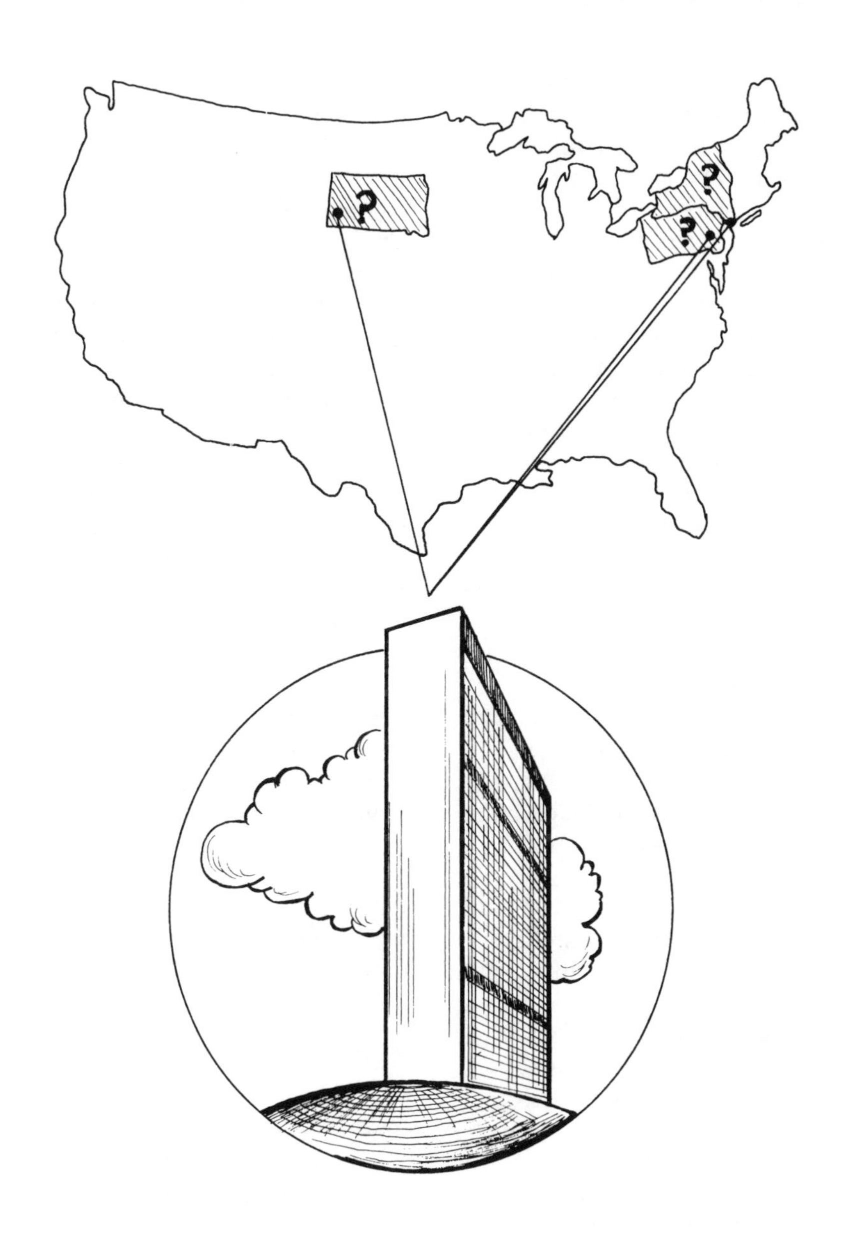

Colossal Capital City was Planned

In 1945 the Black Hills was proposed as a site for world headquarters of the United Nations. The architect Luvine Berg was hired to plan a Black Hills dream city for the U.N.

From Berg's blueprints and drawings we can trace his vision of one Black Hills valley transformed into a world capital. That valley is still known as America Center, because for Berg it was the center of North America. America Center is three miles east and two miles north of Custer.

Berg designed a map to prove the Black Hills were the most interior spot on the continent, and the most remote from oceans. A big circle on the map touches the Pacific, Gulf of Mexico, and Hudson's Bay, and has as its center the Black Hills. In every direction, it is 1,100 miles to a salt water sea.

Berg planned a colossal United Nations headquarters at America Center. His drawings show spiral avenues, some 170 feet wide and lined with embassies of all nations, ending in a massive capitol building. This capitol building was to have a million square feet of office space, and a 20,000 seat auditorium. Atop its 30th story sat a huge globe.

Berg felt the many peaceful Black Hills canyons would allow for exclusive national villages. He wrote of his plan as being "...so colossal a place that it may well accommodate the capital of Jupiter."

A bizarre three-dimensional model of the planned city gathers dust in Berg's former studio. That studio is located, of course, at America Center.

Another post-war scheme called for a World Highway, which Berg worked into his city plan as the main street. This highway would have passed near the Hills in connecting South Africa with Argentina! The only gap in the highway was to have been the Bering Straits separating Russia and Alaska.

But neither the World Highway nor the Black Hills U.N. was ever built. This despite the efforts of Luvine Berg and Paul Bellamy—men who dared to dream the biggest Black Hills dream ever.

Based on a drawing by Luvine Berg.

Fort Held Prisoners of War

A little known final chapter in the Indians vs. U.S. Cavalry story occurred 16 years after Wounded Knee! In 1906 Ft. Meade's cavalry helped capture 400 "renegade" Ute Indians. These Indians had abandoned their ever-shrinking Utah reservation to seek a better life and possible alliance with South Dakota's Sioux.

The Utes embarked on a strange odyssey through Utah, Wyoming and Montana. They caused little trouble, other than alarming ranchers by subsisting on beef cattle. But bloodshed was anticipated. Cavalry troops from Ft. Meade and three other forts were dispatched to bring the Utes to Ft. Meade. The Indians and soldiers made a caravan two miles long, which snaked through the streets of Belle Fourche and Sturgis. School was dismissed for this "parade."

The Utes were instructed to camp at a site across from the present Black Hills National Cemetery and there they remained as virtual prisoners for eight months. In 1907, an effort was made to relocate the Utes on a corner of the Cheyenne River Reservation near Thunder Butte.

Forty years later, another group of prisoners was detained at the Fort. Two hundred troops of General Rommel's African Corp were brought there to work in the sugar beet fields around Belle Fourche. Each evening the POWs were trucked to a barbed wire compound at Ft. Meade, their home from the fall of 1944 until late 1945.

German soldiers on the African front were older men, for Hitler's younger and stronger combatants fought in Europe. The Old World masonry and carpentry skills of these elder soldiers were used to accurately restore Ft. Meade's original buildings.

Was This Lost City of the Ancients?

When people heard that an ancient walled city lay beneath a Black Hills cow pasture, they couldn't believe it! But excavation of such a site began in 1927. It was called Hidden City, and there workers unearthed an apparently man-made stone wall 1,200 feet long. They also uncovered the cobblestones of a street or courtyard, something that looked like an archway, and an unusual rock with marks thought to be hieroglyphics. Between the stones was mortar-like material.

Hidden City's discoverer was C.H. Reich. He had been plowing a hillside five miles south of Rapid City when his plowshare uncovered part of a stone wall. Reich took one of the stones to a fortune-teller, who told him the stone was somehow connected to a "temple of gold." Since the stone wall merged into the hillside, some speculated that the hill might conceal such a temple.

Tourists flocked to Hidden City. Among the curious was President Calvin Coolidge. The President was so impressed with the "ruins" that he later sent his son. Another of the visitors was a Swedish archaeologist, who stated, "This could not possibly be a natural formation." He and others pointed to the straightness of the walls, and the right angles. In Minneapolis and Chicago, people wanted to know more. If proven true, the discovery would rewrite many pages of history.

From the start, there were skeptics. "The whole thing may be some freak of nature," wrote the *Rapid City Journal* on May 23, 1927. Then geologists from the South Dakota School of Mines passed their verdict. What they found was not the sole surviving remnant of a "hidden city," but a natural, though very unusual series of sandstone "dikes."

So Hidden City was definitely not man-made. But the curious still lined up to pay their 50 cent admission. Whatever Hidden City was, people wanted to see for themselves. By the early 1930s it was the top tourist attraction in the Black Hills.

Then things went sour for Hidden City. The big museum building burned to the ground. And traffic that had gone to Mt. Rushmore via nearby Highway 79 was shifting over to Highway 16. Hidden City closed some time before World War II. Today a visitor would see only the museum chimney, evidence of excavation, and a few curious rocks. All else has been reburied.

Waterfalls Add to Hills Mystique

You can hike all over the Black Hills and still not see the three best waterfalls. That's because one is lost, one is buried in a mountain, and one is bone dry!

The lost waterfall is Forsyth Falls. It was photographed on George Custer's 1874 Expedition. But the whereabouts of this 45 foot cataract has never been determined. All we have is the old photo, which is reproduced in at least two history books. See it on page 199 of Krause and Olson's *Prelude to Glory*, or on page 142 of Don Progulske's *Yellow, Ore, Yellow Hair, Yellow Pine*.

The next "missing" waterfall is really very easy to find—because Thunderhead Falls, though 600 feet inside a mountain, is today a tourist attraction. This falls is man-made and part of a century-old tunnel built for mining gold. The waters of Rapid Creek roar through the tunnel and over a 32-foot precipice. This creates the underground falls. The falls became a tourist stop in 1950 but before that, it had been all but forgotten.

Spearfish Falls is bone dry. But when water cascaded down its face the sight was enough to halt excursion trains near Savoy in Spearfish Canyon. The tracks of the Burlington Line ran almost over the top of this falls, nicknamed "Baby Niagara." Old photos show trains stopped while passengers peer out the windows and down the nearly 60 feet of waterfall.

Spearfish Falls was the biggest waterfall in the Hills. It stopped running in 1917. That's when Homestake Company diverted the waters of Little Spearfish Creek into a hydroelectric pipeline.

Go up Little Spearfish Creek and you'll find Roughlock Falls. And in frontier times, this was the site of a steep wagon road. Covered wagons descending the road had only one way to apply the brakes—by chaining wagon wheels together. Muleskinners called this braking a "roughlock," which gave the falls its name.

302

Cavalry Cemetery is an American Original

The Cavalry Post Cemetery at Fort Meade is one of a kind. It is American's only original cavalry post cemetery that hasn't been relocated. For over 100 years, this cemetery has occupied the same pine-covered ridge south of the Fort. Its tombstones tell many stories.

One of the graves is of William Fool Soldier, Company L, 3rd Cavalry. He gained his unusual name in a legendary act of heroism known to few. Here is that story—

Fool Soldier and ten other Teton Sioux became heros in 1862 near present-day Mobridge. There they overtook a renegade band of Santee Sioux who had earlier captured two white women and seven children. The Tetons, all teenage volunteers for this rescue mission, demanded freedom for the captives. They eventually had to trade many personal possessions to gain release of the hostages. The young Tetons were never repaid for their losses. Because of this, they were known ever after as the "Fool Soldiers."

Albert Knaak, a sergeant and Swiss immigrant, was buried there in 1897. It was not until years later that Fort historians rediscovered that Knaak was a recipient of the country's highest military honor. Knaak then received a new tombstone, which listed his Congressional Medal of Honor.

Further on in the cemetery is a nine-foot-tall monument erected by the hard-drinking enlistees of Troop D, 8th Cavalary. It honors two of their group who, legend has it, died after drinking too much wood alcohol while on patrol.

Another grave, marked simply "Laundress," is believed to belong to "Ma" Nash. She had been connected with the laundry business of one fort or another for years, and had been married more than once. "Ma" Nash seemed ordinary enough, except she wore a veil and had insisted that when her time came, she be buried without a fuss. Death came in 1879. People may have wondered what to put on the gravestone, for it turned out that "Ma" Nash was really a man!

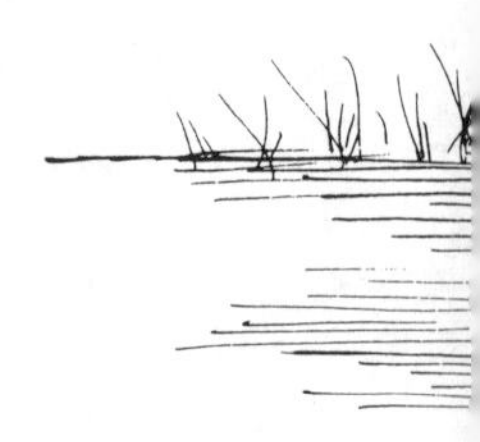

Indians Defend Badlands "Castle"

The last refuge, the final fortress of a nation is marked by neither monument nor marker. It is a badlands mesa known as the Stronghold. The Stronghold was where Sioux Indians made their last stand for a nomadic lifestyle, yet the site is not even listed on maps.

The Stronghold gained a place in history in 1890, just before the tragedy at Wounded Knee. Many events of that year can be traced to a spiritual revival known as the Ghost Dance or Messiah movement. This movement predicted a mystical return to a world with buffalo, and without white settlers. Ghost Dance followers began slipping away from reservations, where the new religion had been forbidden. A thousand followers set out to find a secluded place to dance the Ghost Dance and await the new world.

Such a place was the Stronghold, fifteen miles southwest of Scenic. This curious formation was so remote that few whites knew of it. The walls of the Stronghold drop 300 feet into the badlands. One can reach the broad top only by first ascending Cuny Table, then crossing a narrow neck of land just wide enough for a wagon. On this "bridge" of land, a few armed men could defend against hundreds. Here the Indians dug shallow rifle pits or trenches still visible today. The Stronghold was truly a natural fortress, complete with gurgling springs and abundant grass.

Some historians feel that Big Foot and his band were enroute to the Stronghold when they died at Wounded Knee. Sitting Bull had similar plans when he was killed by reservation police trying to arrest him.

The U.S. Army labeled Indians on the Stronghold as "hostiles." But no effort was ever made to take the Stronghold by force, even though western South Dakota was then surrounded by the largest peace-time concentration of troops in the history of the frontier. Indians eventually abandoned their windswept mesa because of severe winter weather.

Cavalry patrols spent the remaining winter months in maneuvers to keep Indians away from the Stronghold. Today this natural fortress is a forgotten monument to a proud people.

Unknown Man First Yelled "Gold!"

The Black Hills were one of the last unmapped, unexplored corners of America when the Custer Expedition arrived in 1874. Men of that expedition "discovered" gold on French Creek. But had gold really been discovered long before 1874? That's one of history's unanswered questions.

The most dramatic evidence of early mining is the Thoen Stone. This rock was found by Spearfish stonemason Louis Thoen in 1887. On it is scratched this sad message:

"Came to these hills in 1833 seven of us DeLacompt, Ezra Kind, G. W. Wood, T. Brown, R. Kent, Wm. King, Indian Crow. All died but me Ezra Kind. Killed by Ind. beyond the high hill, got our gold in 1834. Got all gold we could carry, our ponys all got by Indians. I have lost my gun and nothing to eat and Indians hunting me."

When Kind wrote this message and concealed it he was hiding on Lookout Mountain, and the "high hill" seems to refer to Crow Peak. Lookout Mountain is immediately north of the Interstate at Spearfish. Crow Peak is the dominant summit just west of town.

Not everyone believes the Thoen Stone is authentic. But there's other evidence of early mining, such as the 1927 letter to the editor from Dr. V. McGillycuddy. This letter, published in the *Rapid City Journal*, states that McGillycuddy was attached to a military exploration unit in 1875. "We found a very old, abandoned cave near what would later be Rapid City," wrote McGillycuddy. In that cave were found "...a rusted frying pan, an old shovel with the handle decayed, and the rusted frame of a pair of spectacles." These items appeared to easily predate Custer's visit. McGillycuddy also found a decayed and moss-covered log cabin on a peak near Sundance. A similar cabin was found on Elk Creek, but with a pine tree growing through the roof!

Probably the first white men to see the Hills were the French explorers, Francois and Joseph Verendrye. Their sketchy journal seems to indicate they entered the Northern Hills on New Year's Day, 1743. The Verendryes may have done a little gold prospecting, but their real search was for the mythical Northwest Passage.

Got all of the
gold we could
carry our ponys
all got by the Indians
I hav lost my gun
and nothing to
eat and indians
hunting me

Relic Art Reveals Primitive Past

Primitive cave drawings and pictographs can be found in the Black Hills. The drawings may have been the work of Asiatic wanderers who roamed the Hills 10,000 years ago. Other pictographs could be less than 150 years old—the art of Plains Indians in the 1800s.

Most drawings on the stone walls of the Black Hills are of deer, buffalo, and antelope. There are also occasional human figures and hard-to-decipher symbols. The most puzzling pictograph in the Black Hills is the so-called "Coronado Map." Located in Red Canyon north of Edgemont, this three foot by five foot map-like drawing was thought by some to be connected with the Spanish explorer and his search for a fabled city of gold. That theory was dismissed by the University of South Dakota's W. H. Over in his unpublished study of pictographs. Over's research uncovered dozens of pictograph sites across the state, and Over hesitates to guess at meanings for the drawings.

Another unusual group of pictographs are found at Ludlow Cave, 80 miles north of the Black Hills. General Custer found and named the site in 1874. Custer's Indian scouts attached great spiritual importance to this cave, saying that wild animals appeared there in a transformed state. This may have been in reference to drawings of antelope and buffalo found on the cave's walls. Custer also found a group of drawings that greatly puzzled him. "I cannot account for the drawings of ships," he wrote in a letter to his wife.

Many Indian relics were found in Ludlow's Cave as might be expected. But unexpected was the discovery of a human skull pierced by a bullet, an old flintlock pistol, and a gold ring with the initials "A.L." These finds perplexed members of the expedition, who thought of themselves as the first white explorers of the area.

Indian scouts told of a legend connected with Ludlow Cave. They believed that from time to time an old man with a long white beard appeared at the cave. This man, according to tradition, had been seen through the generations and was "...without beginning of days or end of years."

Bandits Feared This "Human Bloodhound"

Boone May was a bounty hunter and a hired gun, and bandits feared him like he was a human bloodhound. His reckless exploits should have meant a place in history equal to Wild Bill Hickok or Calamity Jane. But today the story of Boone May is one of the great forgotten sagas of the Old West.

Take the time when Boone May was escorting the Cheyenne-Deadwood Stage. At a place called Robber's Roost on the Cheyenne River, the stage was ambushed. May was riding rear guard, but came galloping to the rescue by shooting dead the bandit Frank Towle. Towle was buried on the spot.

Only later did May discover Cheyenne City was offering a reward for any man bringing in Towle, dead or alive. But since Cheyenne was over two hundred miles away, May balked at the idea of taking a corpse that distance on horseback. Instead, May dug up the body, chopped off the head which he put in a sack, and rode off to collect the reward.

At Cheyenne, May rolled the skull onto the desk of a startled official. But no reward was paid, as the bounty had been lifted. May carried his ghastly trophy around for days in a vain effort to collect bounty.

One year after this event, Boone May helped track down an outlaw named Curly Grimes. Grimes was no ordinary criminal. He was the fastest gun, some said, west of the Missouri.

May helped capture Grimes on Elk Creek, and was escorting the prisoner to Sturgis when an escape attempt was made. According to May, Grimes had asked that his handcuffs be removed because of sub-zero temperatures. Shortly thereafter, Grimes made his break for freedom, and was shot in the back. But because Boone May had a "trigger happy" reputation, he was indicted for murder. A jury settled the issue with a "not guilty" verdict. Curly Grimes was buried where he fell, across the Interstate from Black Hills National Cemetery.

Boone May became a major character in "*A Sole Survivor*," a collection of tales by Ambrose Bierce. (May's exploits were also chronicled by Edgar Beecher Bronson). Bierce met May in 1880 and hired him to protect gold taken from the Rockerville Flume project. When there was criticism for hiring a man still under indictment for the Grimes killing, a defiant Bierce made this entry on the payroll: "Boone May—Murderer."

Stagecoach robbers feared no one more than Boone May. But with the coming of railroads, May's bold talents were no longer required. He drifted down to South America where he found a new frontier and another chance to chase desperados.

Wild Horses Roamed Badlands for Years

As recently as the early 1960s, a few people were lucky enough to see wild horses in the Badlands.

These wild horses, the last in South Dakota, were all descendents of ranch mounts that either escaped or were turned loose by their bankrupt owners. The number of "outlaw" horses increased in the Twenties and Thirties as many homesteaders abandoned their holdings.

By 1928, a large herd of feral horses roamed the open range east of Interior. This was the Runyan Herd, the fleet offspring of race horses once owned by a settler named Runyan. During the Depression, hundreds of these horses were rounded up and sold by county officials desperate for revenue.

To catch a speedy Runyan horse, or any other wild horse, was the goal of many a young cowboy. A horse born in the wild was unbranded, and usually considered the fair property of whoever could lasso or corral it. This was no easy task.

Badlands horses were famed for their ability to elude capture. At a dead run, they could disappear among pinnacles and peaks, then reappear minutes later where least expected. Their knowledge of escape routes was uncanny.

The last area for wild horses was the Lost Dog Country, so named because even a dog could get lost among its many gullies. And just like a movie script, the last herd of fifteen mares was led by a black stallion. This stallion, like those before him, was often blamed for "stealing" mares off area ranches.

In 1959, Lynn Williams of Wall, used his airplane to herd what may have been the last three wild horses past a group of camping Boy Scouts. At this time, the Park Service was attempting to remove all horses from the Badlands Monument. There is no record of when the last capture was made, but on that day, wild horses thundered into the pages of South Dakota history.

SUSAN TURNBULL

Boot Hill Tells Silent Story

The slopes of Deadwood's "Boot Hill" hold the graves of famous and not-so-famous frontier figures. Here are the final resting places of Wild Bill Hickok, Calamity Jane, and Preacher Smith. Beyond is the Chinese section, where every grave lies open and empty. Were the people of Deadwood's once thriving Chinatown the victims of a mass grave robbery? Here's the real story:

Nineteenth century Chinese immigrants to the American West retained much of their oriental lifestyle. One vital custom for the pigtailed laundrymen and laborers of Deadwood's Chinatown involved reburial in the homeland. Thus arrangements were always made for the eventual removal of Deadwood's Chinese dead to the land of the ancestors.

The Chinese initally buried their deceased on Boot Hill, known locally as Mount Moriah. After a sufficient passage of time the bones were disinterred. Then each bone was individually wrapped in muslin and placed in a narrow, metal-lined box. The box was afterwards shipped to mainland China. A guarantee for this reburial was often written into the contracts which initally brought the Chinese to America. This is why today all that remains of the Chinese plots on Mount Moriah are caved-in spots in the ground.

Index